Backing Up 101

Six Different Ways to Back Up Your Computer, and Which Ones You Should Use

V 1.02

by

Leo A. Notenboom

An Ask Leo!® book

https://askleo.com

ISBN: 978-1-937018-16-0

Table of Contents

The Ask Leo! Manifesto

I believe personal technology is essential to humanity's future.

It has amazing potential to empower individuals,
but it can also frustrate and intimidate.

I want to make technology work for you.

I want to replace that *frustration* and *intimidation*
with the *amazement* and *wonder* that I feel every day.

I want it to be a *resource* rather than a *roadblock*;
a *valuable tool,* instead of a source of *irritation*.

I want personal technology to empower you,
so you can be a part of that amazing future.

That's why Ask Leo! exists.

Leo A. Notenboom
https://askleo.com

First: A Freebie for You

Before we dive in, I have something for you: my Ask Leo! special report, "**10 Reasons Your Computer is Slow (and what to do about it)**". This report will help you identify why your computer is slowing down, and take the steps you can to fix it.

It's yours free when you subscribe to my weekly Ask Leo! newsletter.

Each week, you'll find fixes to common problems, tips to keep your computer and online information safe and secure, commentary on technology issues of the day, and even the occasional explanation as to just why things are the way they are. It's educational and fun, and can help you be more effective and less frustrated as you use technology.

And it's completely FREE.

Visit https://go.askleo.com/news101 to learn more, browse the archives, and sign up, today!

Be Sure To Register Your Book!

Your purchase of this book entitles you to several additional free bonuses.

- All available digital formats of the book as direct downloads, so that regardless of which version you purchase, you can enjoy this book on the digital device of your choice.

- Digital updates for life.

- Errata and prioritized Q&A.

You'll find the information that you need to register in a chapter near the end of the book. Once you register, you'll be taken to a web page that will list all available bonuses.

Introduction: Backing up and you

It's been said that, much like dieting, the best backup is any backup you'll actually do.

Also like dieting, we all know we *should* back up, but many of us find excuses: it's too complicated, it's too much work, I don't know what to do...

My favorite back-up excuse? "I've never needed one before."

When it comes to backups, trust me, you will. The only person who's never needed a backup is a person who's new to computing. Eventually, it happens to us all.

There are as many different ways to back up your data as there are ways to lose weight, and all have their pros and cons.

The scariest part is that depending on your choice, you might not be as doing it as well as you think you are. (I'm talking backups here, although I'm sure the same applies to losing weight as well.)

So how do you figure out which kind of backup you need?

That's what this book is all about.

I'll present an overview of the various types of backups, what they cover, what they don't, and what you need to consider when selecting your approach to backing up.

Nothing, and I do mean nothing, can save you from almost any computer disaster like a proper and recent backup.

This book is all about defining "proper" for you and your computer.

What is a backup?

A backup is a duplicate copy of some or all of the files on your computer, kept in a safe place. Nothing more, nothing less.

Backing up is the process of making a backup.

The goal of backing up is very simple: if something happens to your computer that prevents you from getting your files—*which happens much more often than people realize*—you can always get the information you need from the backup.

Where backing up can begin to seem complicated is in the myriad of options relating to what to back up, how often to back up, where to back up, and the various tools that make sure that all that happens regularly... not to mention the multitude of *opinions* on the matter.

Backing up typically takes one of two forms:

- Copying your data. This is a very simple concept. For example, if you copy pictures from your digital camera and burn those pictures to a CD for safe-keeping, you've backed them up. Similarly, if you regularly take the contents of your My Documents folder tree, and copy it to another machine or burn it to CD, that's also a form of backing those files up. They're safely stored in another location *in addition* to the original.

- Copying your system. This is also conceptually simple: rather than backing up only this and that, and hoping you actually remembered to include everything you might need in case of a disaster, this approach makes a copy of *everything*: your data, your programs, your settings—even the operating system itself.

Both types of backups share a common characteristic: whatever they backup—be it just certain files and folders, or absolutely everything—they do so by a) making a copy and then b) placing that copy somewhere else.

If your data is in only one place (meaning there are no other copies), you're not backed up.

Let's see what that looks like, and why it might (rarely) even be the right thing.

Backup type 1: No backup at all

Mary got a new computer about six months ago. She's been very pleased with it, and has been using it almost every day. She uses Outlook, from Microsoft Office, as her email program, and keeps all of her email, documents, and much more on the machine.

In fact, Mary's quite proud of herself, as she's figured out how to move pictures from her digital camera to her computer so she can edit them. She's actually quite the whiz at PhotoShop and has received many "Ooooh, how did you do that?" kind of comments from her friends and family.

Mary has a lot invested in her computer.

Unfortunately, Mary hasn't gotten around to setting up any kind of backup. She's been so busy with her life that the hassle of setting up a backup was something she just kept putting off.

Yesterday, her computer wouldn't boot at all. For reasons unknown, the computer simply wouldn't respond.

She took it to a technician, who gave her some absolutely devastating news: the hard drive in the machine had suffered a catastrophic failure and could not be repaired. All the data on it was lost.

All her photos, email, documents ... everything ... were gone in an instant.

She had no backup at all.

Believe it or not, there are situations in which no backup at all is appropriate. Those situations usually involve cases where total and complete data loss is inconsequential.

My guess is that *inconsequential* isn't a word that you'd use often when it comes to total data loss, which is why this is rarely a good idea. Unfortunately, it's not a rare situation.

Indeed, I myself have two or three machines that are not being backed up at all.

Yes, me.

The important point is that this is a *conscious decision* I'm making, **not** simple neglect. The data on these machines is completely replaceable (so in a sense, it *is* backed up). Should there ever be a catastrophic failure, I'll choose to reinstall the system software and data. Rather than take the time and space required to set up and maintain an ongoing backup, *as there would be no data loss,* I'm choosing to accept the pain of a re-install later if it is ever actually needed.

If you choose not to backup, do it only as a well-thought out decision, not because you never got around to it.

As I said, not being backed up *at all* is frighteningly common. Many people don't take the time to consider that perhaps their computer, camera, smartphone, tablet, or other device might not be indestructible. It never occurs to them that something can go wrong and all of their precious data can be destroyed in the blink of an eye—until, of course, it does.

99.99% of the time, having no backup at all is *completely unacceptable* if you're at all interested in preserving your information and perhaps even your entire system.

On the other hand, you are reading this book. You're already convinced. Let's start backing up.

No backup: When it makes sense

Never—unless you've really thought through the issues and understand the ramifications *completely*.

No backup: When it doesn't make sense

99.9999% of the time. Don't do this.

Backup type 2: Manual file backup

Peter has had his laptop for a while. In fact, he's kind of an old pro at using his computer, and has become an informal resource for many of his friends and family when it comes to computer problems.

Peter has lots of experience with different computer programs, most of which are installed on his computer. He uses some daily and others not so much, but he can quickly research any problem he comes across, because he has so much ready to go on his machine.

After accidentally deleting a file some years back, Peter developed the habit of copying whatever he's working on to a flash drive as a backup copy, just in case he ever makes that same accidental deletion mistake again.

Yesterday, Peter took his computer to Starbucks, where he spent a very productive afternoon working on a memoir he's compiling. Normally, he'd copy the work to his thumb drive, but today, for some reason, he couldn't find it.

At one point, he went to the restroom, and when he came back, he discovered that his laptop had been stolen.

While the thumb drive (which he would later find at home in his other pants) had a copy of the memoir as it was before his trip to the coffee house, the entire afternoon of work was lost.

In addition to setting up and reconfiguring his replacement machine a few days later, he then spent several days reinstalling all of the software that he had been using on the machine that had been stolen. He also came to realize that he had not been backing up some important files as often as he should have been.

Peter was backing up manually, and had missed several important things.

As I said, a backup is nothing more than a *copy* of something kept *somewhere else*.

One approach is to do that manually.

By that, I mean you periodically remember to copy files from your computer to somewhere else—a USB stick, an external hard drive, or to the cloud.

It's absolutely better than nothing. But backing up manually is totally dependent on:

- You remembering to do it.

- You remembering what files you need to back up, *every time*.

Now, I don't know about you, but my memory is nowhere near what it used to be, and certainly not even close to what it would take for this to be an acceptable backup strategy.

But it doesn't take a bad memory for a manual backup process to end up a failure. Not knowing all the files that should be backed up is perhaps the most common problem following unexpected disasters such as hardware failure or theft (or the all-too-common situation where the computer *and the backup* are forgotten or stolen at the same time).

Manual file backup: When it makes sense

There are scenarios where manual backups are the only option. The most compelling is when you're using someone else's computer—particularly a shared computer resource of some sort.

In cases where you're actually working on data stored on another person's computer, you probably won't have the ability to apply some of the techniques that I'll be talking about shortly. The only reasonable recourse you may have is to carry around a flash drive and make a copy of your data then and there. In fact, because you can't rely on the shared computer *at all,* you should probably carry two flash drives—one and a backup.

Manual file backup: When it doesn't make sense

99% of the time. Don't rely on this unless it's the only choice.

Backup type 3: Automatic file backup

Mark knows about backups. Ever since he lost the only copy of his master's thesis some years ago, he's been fanatical about backing up his data.

By getting a backup program and configuring it to back up the contents of his My Documents folder automatically to an external drive nightly, he's relatively certain that he's safe from major catastrophes. In fact, he also saves those backups for a while, moving them to another computer when the external drive he's using fills up.

If his hard drive fails or he accidentally deletes important work, he can recover the most recently backed-up copy from his external drive (or that other computer, although those backups will be a tad older).

*What Mark **isn't** backing up is his system and installed programs, as well as any files he cares about that aren't somewhere within My Documents. Fortunately, many programs use My Documents as the default storage location, so he's actually in pretty good shape when it comes to things he might be working on.*

Unfortunately, when his system finally crashes and wipes out the hard disk, everything that was in My Documents at the time of the last backup is all he has. Mark now has to go through the process of reinstalling his operating system and all applications from scratch, and hope that there wasn't anything important that he would have wanted outside of My Documents.

It's not as common as it once was, but many backup programs will actually default to backing up only contents of a select set of folders on your machine. My Documents, the default location for documents, music, and a variety of other things, is naturally at the top of the list.

This can be a good backup strategy, if you understand what is *not* getting backed up:

- Windows itself is not getting backed up.

- Your installed programs are not getting backed up.

- Any settings or customizations that you've made to Windows, or those programs, is not getting backed up.

- Any files not within My Documents, or any other folders backup programs might default to, are not getting backed up.

That might actually be OK. In the case of total system failure, the risk that you run is that you'll need to reinstall or recreate all of the things that weren't getting backed up.

In the case of other types of failures—such as accidental deletions, for example—an automatic file backup fits the bill quite nicely. It often represents a good trade-off between backing up your important files, and the amount of space those backups might take up over time, versus the cost of reinstalling everything in the worst-case scenario.

Automatic file backup: When it makes sense

Automatically backing up your important data files is what I'd consider a bare minimum backup. It makes sense when you know that all of your files are in the backed-up locations, and you don't mind setting up your system from scratch in the event of a catastrophic failure.

It might also make some sense if you're low on backup space, as backing up your entire system will take up more space. I'll talk more about that in the next section. If space on your system is the factor leading to this decision, however, I'd encourage the purchase of a larger backup drive.

Automatic file backup: When it doesn't make sense

Backing up only your data sounds great until you actually have that catastrophic failure. For example, if you don't have the original installation media for Windows, then backing up your files isn't enough. A replacement hard drive won't come with Windows pre-installed, and you'll then have to take extra steps— and often expense—to get a copy of Windows to reinstall.

Similarly, if the loss of all of your settings and customizations (such as email configuration, bookmarks and the like) would be a problem for you, then backing up only your data files isn't enough.

Backup type 4: Automatic online file backup

Like many of us, Susan uses her computer for assorted tasks, including writing documents for work: long documents, complex documents, and even long, complex documents.

Also like many of us, Susan likes to use the camera in her mobile phone to take pictures. It's convenient, it's always with her, and since the quality of the cameras is good for casual photography, she feels she needs nothing more.

Susan also uses more than one computer. She has one at work, and both a desktop and a laptop at home. And of course, she has her cellphone.

Susan uses Dropbox to keep files synchronized between her computers. She places her documents into a Dropbox folder as soon as she creates them, and works on them in that folder rather than the default My Documents. That way, regardless of how she's left her work on one computer, her others are automatically up-to-date.

Susan also has Dropbox installed on her phone. She's configured it to upload any photos she takes to her Dropbox folder automatically. That way, they show up on her PC's Dropbox folder, and she doesn't have to worry about the hassle of transferring the files by email or by USB cable.

Susan doesn't know it, or perhaps think of it this way, but she's also automatically backing up her documents.

First, let me clarify one thing: there are several online backup services. They are *exactly* like the automatic backup that I described in the previous section, with one important difference: they store your information somewhere online in the cloud rather than on an external hard disk. The online aspect has pros and cons that are similar to Susan's experience with DropBox, but as to exactly *what* they back up, it's often the exact same set of files that I described above: everything in My Documents, a few other select folders, and nothing more.

I'm using Susan's use of DropBox as an example to show just how easy some level of backup can be. So easy, in fact, you might not even know that it's happening.

One excellent technique to leveraging a tool like DropBox is to change the default document folder for your applications to be a folder within your Dropbox folder. For example, you might change the default document folder in Microsoft Word from My Documents to C:\DropBox\WordDocuments. Now, every document that you create will automatically get copied to the other machines on which you have Dropbox installed.

When you enable the Automatic Photo Uploads setting in Dropbox on your smartphone, it creates a folder called Camera Uploads, and places every photo you take there. As a result, it's automatically copied to the other machines on which you have Dropbox.

Automatic copies. That sounds like a backup to me.

Among Dropbox's other features is web access. Even if you have only one computer on which you install Dropbox, your files are automatically uploaded to Dropbox's server, so you can access those files via the Dropbox website from any computer.

The Dropbox servers are another location that stores a copy of your files. Again, that sounds very much like a backup.

I use Dropbox as the most common example here, but there are now many similar services that can perform this same task and come with varying amounts of storage capabilities for free.

Automatic online file backup: When it makes sense

Much like Automatic File Backup above, this type of backup makes sense when you know that all of your important files are in the backed-up locations, and you don't mind setting up your system from scratch in the event of a catastrophic failure.

This is *exactly* the level of backup that I use for my wife's computer. I've changed the default folders for her word processor and spreadsheet programs to be a folder within our shared Dropbox. Any document that she creates or updates is automatically backed up to several computers in our home and the Dropbox online account.

I actually highly recommend this type of backup in addition to some of the more complete types of backup that I'll be discussing next. The nice thing about a utility like DropBox is that as long as it's connected to the internet it copies in real-time; each time you save or update a file, Dropbox does its thing.

And yes, the very document that is this book sits in a subfolder of my Dropbox folder and gets backed up every time I hit **Save**.

Automatic online file backup: When it doesn't make sense

As your only system for backups, you could face problems if you don't have the original installation media for Windows to reinstall, or if losing files and settings not contained in the backed-up folders would be a hardship.

In addition, online backup may not be appropriate for highly sensitive documents. The services are typically quite secure and reliable, but you have to remember that there are situations where your account could be hacked, making your information accessible to others.

This is extremely rare. In fact, I continue to rely on services like Dropbox daily. But if security is important to you, you may want to use tools like BoxCryptor (specifically designed for utilities like Dropbox) or TrueCrypt to add a layer of encryption.

Background: What's an image?

I have to start by clarifying a term that is used ambiguously and often in conflicting ways.

An *image* is a copy of **everything** on a hard disk.

That seems fairly clear, but some people still have questions.

Does "everything" include all of the empty space on the hard drive? Does it include the left-over data stored in areas of the hard disk that aren't currently in use? Does the image have the exact same physical layout and organization—i.e., fragmented or not?

Some people use the term *image* implying the answers to all of those questions is yes.

I (and others) do not.

What I'll refer to as an **image** is a copy of *all* and *only* the currently-stored data on a hard disk. It includes *every* file, directory entry, boot sector, and file allocation record. Every bit of information that is currently marked as being used becomes part of an image. It does not include data stored in sectors that are marked as empty, and it does not preserve the physical layout of the actual files on the media.

What I would call a **clone** (or perhaps *sector-based image*) includes every sector of data on the hard drive, used or not, and preserves the layout of those sectors.

For backing up your data, a clone is simply not necessary. It has its uses, but the average backup is not one of them.

Images, however, are the single most important approach to backing up.

Backup type 5: Manual image backups

Max just got a new machine.

Unfortunately, Max was unable to obtain Windows Installation discs to accompany it. Windows was preinstalled, and even placed on a recovery partition, but no CDs or DVDs accompanied the machine.

Max has been here before. A few years ago, he actually had to purchase a brand new copy of Windows because his hard disk crashed and he had no installation media to reinstall Windows onto the replacement drive. He'd pleaded with the computer vendor, but they were unsympathetic, so his only recourse was to purchase that replacement copy of Windows.

This time, however, will be different.

After setting up his new machine, Max installs Macrium Reflect's free edition and immediately creates a full system image backup on an external hard drive. That image backup contains everything on the machine, including Windows itself and any other software that came preinstalled.

Max then saves the external hard drive on which he placed that image in a safe place.

Max doesn't realize it now, but in two years, when the hard drive in his computer suffers a catastrophic failure, he'll be very glad that he saved this image, as he'll be able to restore it to the replacement hard drive. That'll effectively put Windows back on the machine in the state it was when he got it.

Taking image backups manually from time to time is a good thing. As Max's story outlines, it's a fantastic way to compensate for not getting an installation DVD for

Windows with your new computer. An image backup simply takes a snapshot of the entire hard disk in its current state, and saves it. Later, when needed, you simply copy that snapshot back to that drive, or a replacement drive, and return the machine back to the exact state it was in at the time the image backup was taken.

The downside of image backups is that they take up space. Note that Max put his image backup onto an external drive of some sort (media such as writable DVDs are simply not big enough to work as practical backup media for images these days). The good news is that external drives—especially ones dedicated to keeping a single image backup—are not particularly expensive.

Taking image backups manually is not necessarily part of a complete backup strategy. Any backup system that relies on your memory is doomed. That's nothing personal, as it applies to all of us, including me. When your system fails and you realize that the last backup that you took manually was months ago, everything since then is lost.

But manual image backups definitely have a place.

Manual image backup: When it makes sense

Max's situation is actually a backup scenario that I heartily recommend. When you get a new machine that doesn't have a system installation disc, make sure to take an image backup as soon as possible. Heck, even if it does come with an installation disc, take that image backup anyway, because should you ever need to, it'll be quicker and easier to restore that backup image than it will be to set Windows up from scratch.

I also recommend that manual image backups be taken at important points in a computer's life—typically right before big changes, or after large updates. For example, I often take a complete image backup of my machine before upgrading my Windows version. Many people take image backups after having installed large software packages or service packs. In all of these cases, the image backup represents a point in time to which you can return your entire machine if something ever goes wrong in the future. It can easily save you the hassle of reinstalling Windows and Windows updates, applications, and more.

Manual image backup: When it doesn't make sense

Manual image backups are not a substitute for ongoing automated backups of some sort.

While any backup is better than no backup, remember that you risk losing everything you've created or changed since the last image backup you took, unless you add an additional kind of backup. That could be as simple as some of the file-based backups I've already discussed, or it could be something as complete (and still pretty simple) as just making image backups automatically and more often.

Let's look at that.

Backup type 6: Automatic image backups

Penny's a pro. No, she's not a professional computer person by any means, but she's had the experience of having been bitten by data loss due to computer failure once or twice in the past. Because of this, she understands the importance of backing up, both regularly and completely.

When she bought her current computer, she also purchased an external hard drive and image backup software. One of the first things she did was set up the backup software to take a complete image backup of her machine every night.

Last week, she accidentally deleted an important file that she needed for work. Using her backup software, she restored a copy of that file from the backup that had been taken the night before.

But that pales in comparison to what happened a couple of months ago. She accidentally opened an attachment in her email that she thought was from a friend. In moments, her machine was infected with malware. In fact, her machine was so badly infected that there was no hope for recovery.

No hope save one. As soon as she realized how bad off the machine was, Penny calmly grabbed her backup software and restored her machine to the backup image taken the night before the infection happened.

Computers are good at doing repetitive tasks automatically, and making image backups is no exception.

As Penny's story outlines, having a complete backup taken for you every night (or day) can be a real lifesaver. The important points of this scenario are very simple:

- By having the computer back itself up daily, you never need to remember to do anything. The computer simply does it all for you—just like we were all promised computers of the future would do!

- By taking an image backup of the entire computer, you can't possibly miss something. Whether you need to recover a single important file, or restore the entire machine, an image backup has it all.

Automatic image backup: When it makes sense

Always.

By far, this is my most recommended solution for most computer users: get and install image backup software, and configure it to back up your machine nightly. If that's too often, you can tweak the dial a little bit and perhaps backup only weekly, but realize that if you need the backup for some reason, it could be as much as a week out of date. Depending on how you use your computer, that may or may not be an issue for you.

If I could get everyone to do this, I'd be a happy man. It's this regular, automatically-scheduled image backup that can save the day nearly every time.

Automatic image backup: When it doesn't make sense

Honestly, an automatic image backup always makes sense. Even on those machines that I choose not to back up, an automated image backup could still add a layer of safety and peace of mind.

If I have to make a case: the biggest arguments against automated image backups might be disk space and timing. When these are an issue, I recommend getting a larger backup drive (believe me, it's worth it) and setting a time. Machines left on 24-hours a day can back up overnight, but machines that are not left on may back up while you're using them. That's typically not an issue. Backups are *so important* that I'd argue it's worth setting up a mechanism where you regularly leave the machine to do its work without interfering with yours.

Again, no arguments against automated image backups—just situations where additional accommodations might be needed. Trust me, they're worth it.

Building on a theme: what's an incremental backup?

One term that gets thrown around a lot when you're dealing with backup software is *incremental backup*. While it's mostly used when discussing image backups, it actually applies to almost any kind of backup, and is essentially what most file-based backups really are.

Here's the deal.

When you back up for the first time, the backup makes a copy of all of files that you're backing up. That's sometimes referred to as a *full backup*.

Now, every time you back up, you could always perform a full backup. That means that the backup you make today actually makes copies of all the files, whether they've been backed up before or not. Again, that's a full backup.

An *incremental* backup takes into account that you've already backed up some files. Rather than making additional copies of all the files, it only copies those files that have changed since the last backup. If no files have changed, then an incremental backup copies nothing. If only one file has changed, then only that one file is copied, and so on.

The big advantage to incremental backups, especially incremental *image* backups, is the reduction in space. A full backup is as big as all of the files being backed up, but an incremental backup taken thereafter is only as big as the files that changed. The net result is that you can keep many more incremental backups on hand than you can full backups, given the same amount of disk space you have for backups.

The downside to incremental backups is that each contains only the files that changed since the previous backup. That means if you need to restore *everything,* you need to start with that initial full backup, and then carefully restore each incremental backup taken thereafter.

The good news is that you rarely need to worry about that process: backup software handles it all automatically. All you need to do is make sure you keep each starting point (the full backup) and all of the incremental backups taken thereafter, until the next starting point.

The bottom line: a summary of my recommendations

Now that you have an idea of the different approaches to backing up, hopefully you'll have a sense of what might apply in your situation. If you make the decision that no backup at all is perfectly OK, then that's fantastic!

I also expect that to be very, very rare.

If you're still not sure, here's my recommendation. When done properly, this will protect you from just about anything that can go wrong:

- Get an image backup program and an inexpensive external hard disk – it only needs to be big enough to hold a single image of your machine – and take an initial system image. Save that external disk somewhere safe until the day you no longer have that machine. You might use it as an alternative if you ever needed to restore to "factory settings".

- Get another external hard disk, probably bigger this time, and configure your image backup program to back it up daily. If you're not sure, do a full backup once a month, followed by daily incremental backups, and keep two months' worth. (Many backup programs can be configured to handle the disk space housekeeping for you automatically.)

- Install a utility like Dropbox and set up a free account. Install it on all your computers if you have more than one.

- Change the default folder for the programs in which you create or manipulate data files, like your word processor or photo editing software, to use a folder you create within your Dropbox folder.

Seriously, that's about it. You'll have nightly backups to protect your system from just about any disaster, along with real-time backups of the files you're working on currently.

And yes, that's how I roll.

Software Mentioned

Let me discuss in a little more detail the software that I've mentioned so far.

Dropbox

I recommend Dropbox because it's the simplest and most feature-rich of the various alternatives. You get two gigabytes of storage for free, and can pay for more if you like. Particularly when it comes to things like documents, it's a good, solid solution.

Other programs come with different capabilities and differing amounts of either free or paid storage. Just a few of those include Google Drive, Amazon Cloud Drive, Microsoft OneDrive, Box.net, SugarSync, SpiderOak, and many others. All provide software you install on your machine to handle automatic synchronization across machines and automatic backup of those files to servers on the internet.

BoxCryptor

BoxCryptor is a fairly unique encryption solution specifically targeted at people who use the tools I just mentioned, and are looking for an extra layer of security. BoxCryptor runs alongside the software on your computer and automatically encrypts the files you place in Dropbox (or other storage system) before they're uploaded to that system's servers. This extra layer of security ensures that only you will be able to access those files, by providing the proper password.

As I mentioned earlier, most file synchronization services and online backup services store your data on their servers in a way that could be compromised by a malicious employee or be retrieved in response to a court order. Doing your own local encryption prevents that.

Macrium Reflect

Macrium Reflect is my backup software of choice. I regularly recommend it. The free version allows you to take full image backups, whereas the paid version (well worth it, in my opinion) adds the ability to schedule backups automatically and perform incremental backups.

There are other alternatives, but I honestly believe that backing up is not a place where you want to skimp. Whatever program you select, make sure it supports:

- Image backups.

- Incremental backups.

- Scheduling.

- The ability to restore individual files extracted from a backup image.

- Its own bootable rescue/restore media.

And of course, you'll want to make sure that the software itself is supported by the company that makes it. This turns out to be a surprising differentiator in the backup software market.

Get more details: My "Saved!" Series

If you want more detailed, step-by-step instructions on exactly how to perform those all-important backups, my "Saved!" series of books is just what you need.

Each book covers specific backup software, and walks you through the steps to:

- Install it (if needed)

- Create that all-important image backup

- Restore an image backup

- Restore individual files from within an image backup

- Test your backup

- Schedule and automate your backup

- Prepare for disaster with rescue media

And more.

The book for my recommended backup solution, Macrium Reflect, is now in its second edition. Saved! Backing Up with Macrium Reflect[1] will help you get your data securely backed up with this professional backup utility.

Other "Saved!" editions cover the backup software included in Windows 7 and 8, and new "Saved!" books are underway to cover even more backup programs.

Backing up is that important.

Each book is available in both paperback and multiple digital formats. Regardless of which format you purchase, *ALL* digital formats are included when you register your purchase at the Ask Leo! Member's site online.

---

[1] https://go.askleo.com/savedm2

Check out the "Saved!" books at The Ask Leo! Store[2].

Afterword

I hope that that this book has helped clear up some of the confusion around backing up, and that you'll now make sure that your data is backed up and safe from all the various things that can go wrong when it comes to computers and the internet.

If you find what you believe to be an error in this book, please register your book and then visit the errata page for this book. That page will list all known errors and corrections, and give you a place to report anything not already listed.

If you're left with questions, suggestions, or—dare I say it—even complaints, then by all means, let me know.

Register your book!

Having purchased this book, you're entitled to additional updates, errata, and other *bonus materials*.

- Regardless of how you purchased this book, you can download this book in any or all of *three digital formats*:

  - **.pdf** (for your computer or any device that can view PDF files)

  - **.mobi** (ideal for the Amazon Kindle)

  - **.epub** (for a variety of other electronic reading devices).

- Other bonuses and supplementary material I might make available in the future.

- Digital updates for life! When I update this book, the digital copies will be available to you to download at will.

Registering gives you access to it all.

Visit:

http://go.askleo.com/regbu101

right now and register. That link is mentioned only here, and it's totally FREE to owners of *Backing Up 101*.

About the Author

I've been writing software in various forms since 1976. In over 18 years at Microsoft, I held both managerial and programming roles in a number of groups, ranging from programming languages to Windows Help, Microsoft Money, and Expedia. Since 2003, I've been answering tech questions at the extremely popular Ask Leo! website (https://askleo.com) and in entrepreneurial projects like this book.

Curious for more? Someone asked and I answered on the site: Who is Leo? (https://askleo.com/who-is-leo/)

Feedback, Questions, and Contacting Leo

I'd love to hear from you.

Honest.

I truly appreciate reader input, comments, feedback, corrections, and opinions—even when the opinions differ from my own!

Here's how best to contact me:

- If you have a comment or a question about this book, I strongly encourage you to register your book, as outlined in above, and use the prioritized comment form in the registered owner's center.

- If you prefer not to register your book, you can email me at leo@askleo.com.

- If you have a computer or tech-related question, the best approach *by far* is to first search Ask Leo! (https://askleo.com). Many, many questions are already answered right there, and finding those answers is much faster than waiting for me.

- If you can't find your answer using Search, visit https://askleo.com/book and submit your question. That's a special form just for book purchasers and it gets prioritized attention.

- If you just want to drop me a line, or have something you want to share that isn't covered above, you can use https://askleo.com/book, or email leo@askleo.com.

- If you're just not sure what to do … email leo@askleo.com. ☺

Copyright & Administrivia

Sharing this Document

The bottom line is that you shouldn't.

More specifically, you shouldn't make copies and give them to others.

Loan your copy as you see fit. (Back it up, of course!) However, making an additional copy to *give* to someone else is a no-no. (The rule is pretty simple: if you *loan* the book, they have access to it, and you shouldn't, until they return it. If both you and your friend can use the book at the same time, then you've made a *copy,* and that's the part that's wrong.) That goes for uploading a copy to an electronic bulletin board, website, file sharing or similar type of service.

The information in this document is copyrighted. That means that giving copies to others is actually *illegal*. But more important than that, it's simply wrong.

Instead, if you think it's valuable enough to share, encourage your friends who need this book to buy a copy of their own. Or, heck, buy one as a gift for them.

Remember, it's the sale of valuable information in books like this one that makes Ask Leo! possible. It's pretty simple, really; if enough people disregard that, there'd be no more books, and eventually no more Ask Leo!

More Ask Leo! Books

If you found this book helpful, check out my growing library of books at https://store.askleo.com.

Use the coupon code BOOKOWNER when you purchase the PDF download version from The Ask Leo! Store at check-out, and get *20% off* the regular price.

The list is always growing, but here are a few of my most popular titles.

⊙

The Ask Leo! Guide to Staying Safe on the Internet

Keep your computer, your data, and yourself safe on the internet.

Every day, we hear about everything from hacked accounts and computers, to viruses, spyware, and other forms of malware, to large data breaches that threaten our online information.

"Internet safety", indeed.

You can use the internet safely!

In this book, I cover the things you must do, the software you must run, and the concepts you must understand to keep your computer and data safe as you use the internet.

⊙

The Ask Leo! Guide to Routine Maintenance

The *Ask Leo! Guide to Routine Maintenance* is all about helping you:

- Keep your computer running longer. There are simple steps you can take, today, to lengthen the useful lifespan of your existing Windows computer.

- Avoid spending money you don't need to spend. By paying attention to some basic maintenance, you can delay unnecessary and often costly upgrades, replacements, and expansions you might not need.

- Speed up your computer. There are things to do, and things to avoid doing, that can keep your computer running as fast as it possibly can, for as long as it possibly can.

- Free up space. Is your disk filling up? There's a good chance that a bunch of it is stuff you don't need. Learn how to identify what to keep and what to trash (and what to back up and *then* trash).

Just Do This: Back Up!

Is this how you feel when faced with thoughts of backing up?

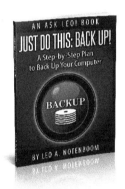

> *"I was immediately so overwhelmed that I gave up."*

> – An Ask Leo! reader

If that sounds too true, then *Just Do This: Back Up* is for you.

Backing up doesn't have to be hard to do. Honest. Making copies of everything important is about as simple as it can be.

The problem is that there are so many options. Each option requires a decision. Each decision requires a choice. Each choice is an opportunity for uncertainty and confusion.

Instead of giving option after confusing option, *Just Do This: Back Up* outlines a step-by-step arrangement for backing up your desktop or laptop PC that just works. Follow these instructions, watch the videos included with the book, and you'll be backed up. You'll be protected against everything from hardware failure to malware infestation, and all the minor-to-major inconveniences in between.

Check out these titles and more at The Ask Leo! Store[3].

---

[3] https://store.askleo.com

www.ingramcontent.com/pod-product-compliance
Lightning Source LLC
La Vergne TN
LVHW080106070326
832902LV00014B/2456